Letters to a Young Pug

WILSON THE PUG WITH NANCY LEVINE

Letters to a Young Pug

Skyhorse Publishing

Visit our website at www.skyhorsepublishing.com.

10 9 8 7 6 5 4 3 2 1

Library of Congress Cataloging-in-Publication Data is available on file.

Cover design by Daniel Lagin
Cover photograph by Nancy Levine

Print ISBN: 978-1-5107-1443-4
Ebook ISBN: 978-1-5107-1447-2

Printed in China

"And as for the rest, let life happen to you. Believe me: life is in the right, always."

—RAINER MARIA RILKE

Introduction

Hello. My name is Wilson the Pug. For those of you who don't know me, here is how I came to be: Long, long ago, around 500 B.C., back when mostly dogs with prominent snouts roamed the Earth, there lived in ancient China my greatest great grandpug, Pug-tzu, as he was called. Perhaps you have heard of him. Pug-tzu was the loyal pug companion of one old wise philosopher, Lao-tzu, who is best known for writing the Tao-te Ching, the ancient Chinese book of wisdom. Wise as he was, it was Pug-tzu who inspired old Lao-tzu to reach his philosophical conclusions and pen the ancient text.

Pug-tzu and Lao-tzu spent many years philosophizing together, until they were both rather gray in the muzzle and long in the tooth. Well, Pug-tzu's teeth were still of the tiny pug goblin variety but, still, he was old.

One day, as they were sitting on a stone bench in their village, or as they called it, "the office," as this was where most of their deep thinking took place, Lao-tzu turned to Pug-tzu and said, "You know, my flat-faced friend, I grow weary of all this philosophizing.

It is hard work. I dream of lounging on the shores of the Yang-tze River, with an empty mind and a full glass. What shall we do?"

Pug-tzu looked deeply into the old man's eyes and cocked his head from side to side, as pugs are wont to do. With this, Lao-tzu had a sudden flash of insight.

"You are so right! *When you have accomplished your goal, simply walk away.* We shall retire!" And he made a mental note to include this nugget of wisdom in his Tao-te Ching.

The pair began making preparations to leave their village and wisdom behind and venture to the banks of the Yang-tze, where they planned to spend their days lounging on her shores with empty minds and full glasses. And bowls.

Lao-tzu took at once to his parchment, penning the Tao-te Ching, working late into the night by candlelight. But Pug-tzu was at a loss. How would he pass along his Taoist wisdom to the next generation of pugs? There was only one other pug in their village. He was known as DimSum. To Pug-tzu, DimSum did not seem a very wise pug at all. He seemed mostly concerned with eating and napping. Still, Pug-tzu had to pass down his wisdom to some puggy, and DimSum was the only game in town.

Pug-tzu worked day and night to school DimSum in the ways of wise Taoist pugs, but still DimSum was mostly interested in food and slumber. Meanwhile, Lao-tzu had all but completed his Tao-te Ching, except for one last thought he was struggling with. He posed his dilemma to Pug-tzu, gazing into his furry companion's huge dark eyes.

"Tell me, how does the Master best teach?"

Pug-tzu just stared at Lao-tzu, cocking his head from side to side, as pugs are wont to do. With this, the old man had an instant realization: "You are so right, my wrinkle-headed friend! *The Master can act without doing anything and teach without saying a word.*" And he turned to scribble this final thought onto his now-complete parchment. With this, it was time to leave the village behind.

On their departure day, Pug-tzu bade adieu to DimSum, promising to write to him every day, continuing their lessons. Lao-tzu and Pug-tzu boarded their buffalo and embarked for the shores of the Yang-tze.

Sure enough, guided by Pug-tzu's letters, DimSum managed to carry on the tradition, in his own way to be sure, imparting the wisdom of the Tao to the next pug in line, down through the ages until it came to rest upon the furry shoulders of my teacher, Otto. Of course, Otto, too, would eventually want to retire, as you shall soon see.

Pug-tzu and Lao-tzu settled on the banks of the Yang-tze, where they lounged away the rest of their days with empty minds and full glasses and bowls. And to this day, if you listen very closely, you can sometimes hear what sounds like a pug snuffle in the river's rushing waters.

—WILSON THE PUG

Letters to a Young Pug

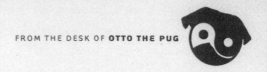

FROM THE DESK OF **OTTO THE PUG**

Dear Wilson,

Though I am old and blind, I can clearly see that the time has come for me to step down and appoint a new Master of our wise Taoist pug lineage. Truth is, I would like very much to retire to a warm beach community in Boca.

As such, the time is ripe to pass the torch to you, my fine young puggly protégé. As is our tradition, you will claim your spiritual inheritance and assume my very comfortable throne. However, in order to do so, you must first complete one last task. Please come visit me at your earliest convenience so I may give you your assignment.

Your gentle Master,
Otto

Dear Wilson,

As we discussed, here is your mission: You must ensure that the next pug in line is ready to take your place. You will be assigned a pupil who must learn our wise ways and thus earn his yin-yang badge. The pug I have chosen for you to initiate is young Homer.

Perhaps you remember Homer from a certain holiday adventure you shared with him. As you can imagine, yours will not be an easy task. Anything worth doing never is. But once Homer earns his yin-yang badge, you will assume the leadership role for which you have been groomed (not merely brushed). And I can spend my days sniffing mah-jongg tiles by the pool.

Now go, go young Wilson, and remember this, as it is written: "The Master can act without doing anything and teach without saying a word."

Your loyal teacher,
Otto

FROM THE DESK OF **WILSON THE PUG**

Dear Homer,

The time has come, my fine young puggly protégé, for you to earn your yin-yang badge.
As you know, we are descended from an ancient and proud tradition of Taoist pugs. You
have been especially chosen to—Homer? Homer? Are you still reading this?

Infinitely and eternally yours,
Wilson

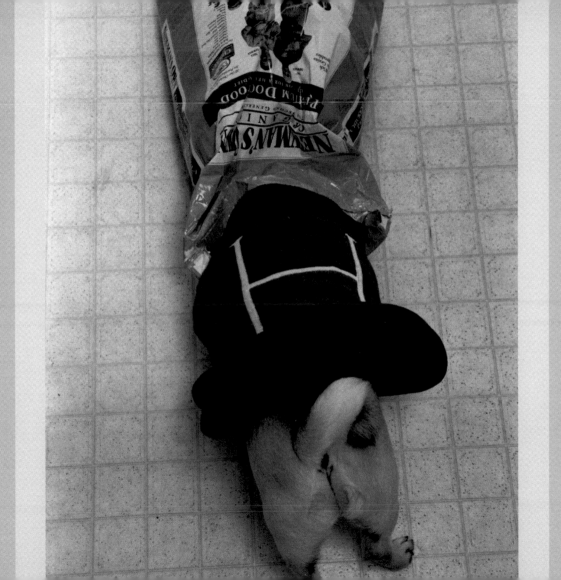

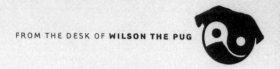

FROM THE DESK OF **WILSON THE PUG**

Dear Homer,

In these letters I will impart all the knowledge of our wise Taoist pug lineage to you, just as Pug-tzu first passed along his wisdom to DimSum and Otto has to me. And one more very important thing—pxasehi;asdkfja;lskgj. Sorry, these keyboards are so small nowadays. More soon.

Eternally yours,
Wilson

FROM THE DESK OF **WILSON THE PUG**

Dear Homer,

I will be mailing you letters daily. This is your first lesson—pugs love mail. Like the Tao, the mail is full of infinite possibility. You will sit by the door and wait for the mail. You will bark at anything that vaguely sounds like mail delivery, even if it's only leaves rustling in the wind. I see the last pickup at this mailbox is at 6 P.M. Do you know what I mean by 6 P.M.?

Infinitely yours,
Wilson

FROM THE DESK OF **WILSON THE PUG**

Dear Homer,

Time is an illusion, and feeding time is the most powerful illusion. It may seem that you spend long hours waiting for kibble to appear in your bowl. And then when it does, it seems to mysteriously disappear. And the bowl is once again empty. But the emptiness is really full of possibility, is it not?

Please send me your thoughts.

Your gentle teacher,
Wilson

FROM THE DESK OF **HOMER THE PUG**

Dear Wilson,

I found your letters today. Getting a yin-yang badge sounds really cool. But that other stuff about infinite possibilities and all? I have to say, I really have no idea what you're talking about.

Party on,
Homer

P.S. But those stamps were delicious. Almost a hint of vanilla. Looking forward to lots more letters!

FROM THE DESK OF **WILSON THE PUG**

Dear Homer,

I sense that you may need a little extra explanation in the ways of the Tao in order to earn your yin-yang badge. The most basic lesson is this: "Being and nonbeing produce each other." When you are just sitting there doing nothing, this is being. Do you know what I mean?

In stillness,
Wilson

FROM THE DESK OF **HOMER THE PUG**

Dear Wilson,

I've gotten a friend to help me who is an expert in beeing. His name is Buzz. Buzz has turned me on to the most outrageous honey you've ever tasted. He made it himself with some help from a flower. I'll tell you one thing—beeing and nonbeeing produce an awesome taste sensation!

Peace out,
Homer

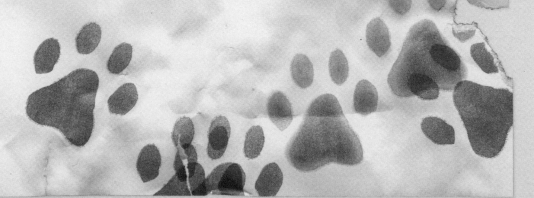

FROM THE DESK OF **HOMER THE PUG**

P.S. Here's Buzz giving me a high five! Now down low . . .

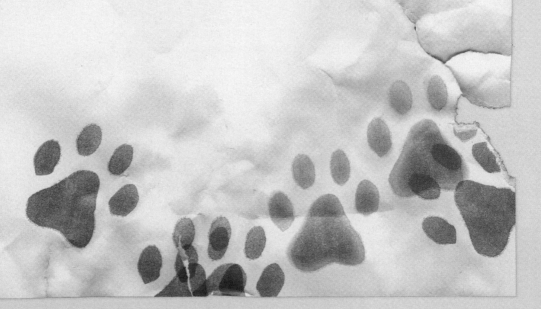

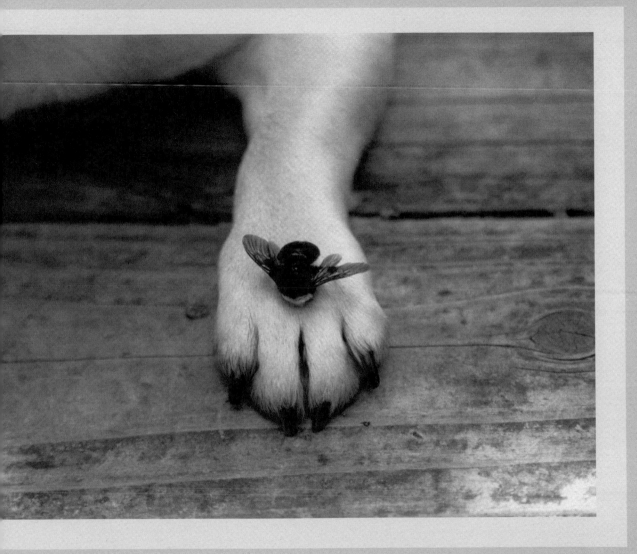

FROM THE DESK OF **WILSON THE PUG**

Dear Homer,

I am thinking my typewritten letters contain too many typos, making them difficult for you to understand. So I have asked my human to take dictation. Here's an important lesson: Your humans will do anything for you. If you look at them just so, tilt your head, open your eyes wide, furrow your brow a little extra, truly, they will comply with your every wish. And thus you will teach them what it is to be free of limitation.

Compassionately yours,
Wilson

FROM THE DESK OF **HOMER THE PUG**

Dear Wilson,

Great suggestion. Check this out: I've found the perfect use for my human.

Just chillin',
Homer

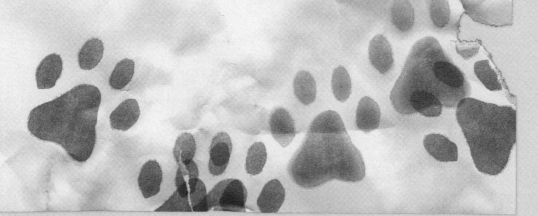

Dear Homer,

It is a fact of pug life—you will be visiting the veterinary office. Like life itself, these visits are filled with mystery and adventure, sometimes pleasant, sometimes not so pleasant. As with all things, best just to embrace the experience.

In truth,
Wilson

Dear Wilson,

I wasn't exactly the one doing the embracing. For some reason, the vet tried to separate my jaw from the rest of my head. I really don't understand his fascination with my tiny goblin teeth anyhow.

Arrgghhh!
Homer

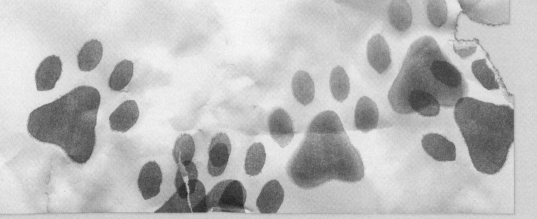

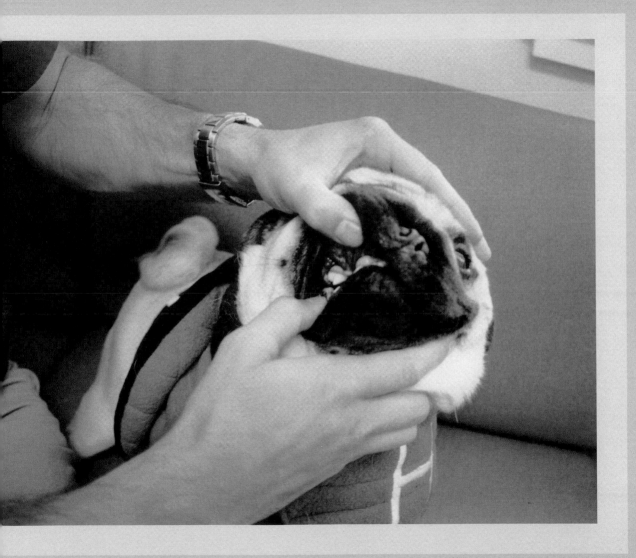

FROM THE DESK OF **HOMER THE PUG**

P.S. Maybe I do understand his fascination with teeth after all. Whatcha got in there, big boy?

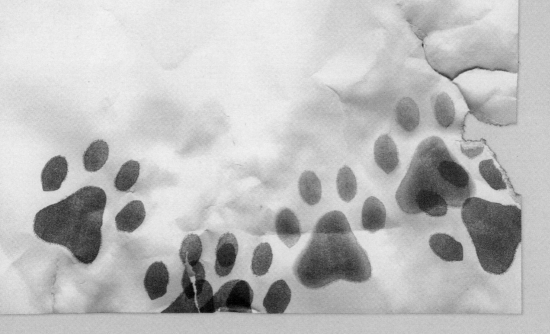

Dear Homer,

A trip to the salon will leave you fluffy and refreshed. But what of this notion of beauty? You will hear people say, "Pugs are so ugly, they're cute." Indulge them this folly as true beauty lies far beyond the mere opposition of ugly and cute.

With kindness,
Wilson

FROM THE DESK OF **WILSON THE PUG**

Dear Homer,

Although pugs are not great fans of washing, if you ever meet a pug who needs a bath, you will appreciate the virtue of cleanliness. And you will come to understand in a very firsthand way how the Tao flows like water.

Patiently yours,
Wilson

FROM THE DESK OF **HOMER THE PUG**

Dear Wilson,

Turns out I'm not really the bath type. Cleanliness, schmenliness. I have a better idea.

I'm out,
Homer

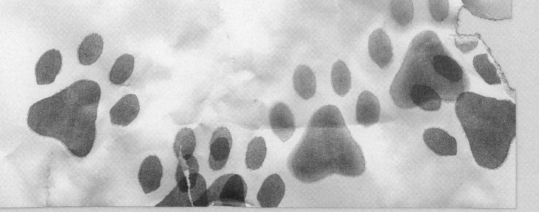

FROM THE DESK OF **HOMER THE PUG**

Dear Wilson,

Now this is more my speedo. And how I'd prefer to cool off on a hot summer day.
I'm prone to overheating, you know. Ah, nothing like a day at the pool.

Ciao for now,
Homer

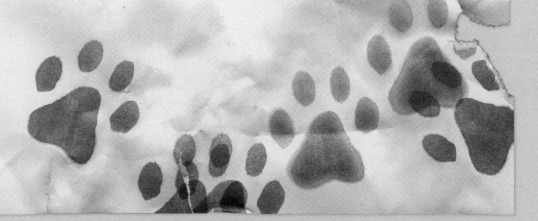

FROM THE DESK OF **WILSON THE PUG**

Dear Homer,

Thank you for your visit. I think our reading sessions will help to facilitate your understanding of the lessons. This book is the definitive modern work on Taoism. As it said in the book—Homer? Homer? Are you still reading this?

In balance,
Wilson

FROM THE DESK OF **HOMER THE PUG**

Dear Wilson,

I prefer watching the definitive modern pug movie on TV. Frank is poetry in motion, dontcha think?

Who let the dogs out?

Woof, woof woof, woof,
Homer

FROM THE DESK OF **WILSON THE PUG**

Dear Homer,

I think it would be best if you didn't spend quite as much time watching TV and instead went out for more walks, as pugs love to do. Personally, I prefer the treadmill as I can walk for miles but go noplace.

Virtuously yours,
Wilson

FROM THE DESK OF **HOMER THE PUG**

Dear Wilson,

I know an easier way of going noplace.

Scchhhhhnnnnnnooooorrrrre . . .
Homer

FROM THE DESK OF **HOMER THE PUG**

Dear Wilson,

While I was napping, I dreamed of a giant bone. I was floating, as if on a cloud, and the giant bone lay in front of me just waiting to be devoured. What do you think my dream means?

Keep it real,
Homer

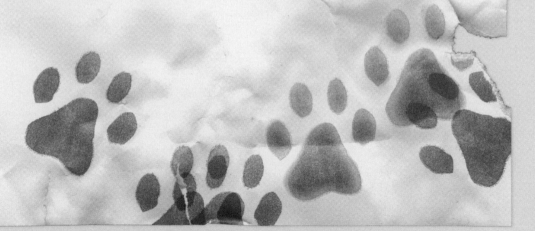

Dear Homer,

I think we can interpret your dream by turning to the definitive modern work on Taoism.
If we look at your dream in terms of the space-time continuum—Homer, were you
listening to this reading?

With calm resolve,
Wilson

FROM THE DESK OF **HOMER THE PUG**

Dear Wilson,

For some reason, while you were reading to me, I fell asleep. I dreamed the giant bone
was in the refrigerator. Right there on the middle shelf. Perfectly chilled, aged to
perfection. Just waiting to be loved.

Mmmmm, giant bone, come to puggy,
Homer

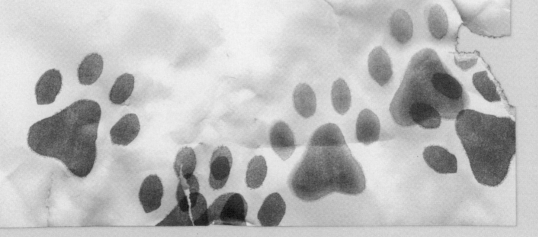

FROM THE DESK OF **WILSON THE PUG**

Dear Homer,

Perhaps you can learn what it is to be a pug by becoming aware of what a pug is not.
For instance, you remember our friend Tater Tot? Tater is not a pug. You may want to
spend some time contemplating what makes a pug and what makes not-a-pug.
(But in doing so, be sure not to interfere or become a distraction.)

With love,
Wilson

FROM THE DESK OF **WILSON THE PUG**

P.S. Here's an example to get you started: Pugs are known for their curly tails. When people ask you why it is that way, don't tell them our secret. Like the Tao itself, let it remain a mystery.

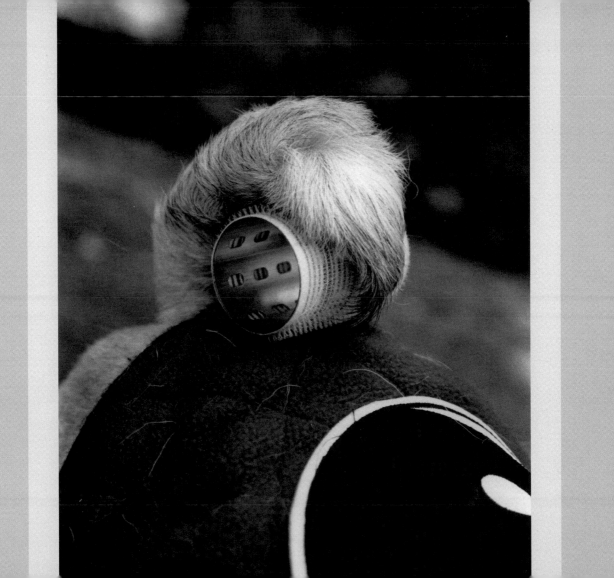

FROM THE DESK OF **HOMER THE PUG**

Dear Wilson,

I know pugs are known for making people laugh. So I wondered, how can I be more amusing? I put on my thinking cap to help me come up with something.

Let's see . . .
Homer

FROM THE DESK OF **HOMER THE PUG**

Dear Wilson,

I realized that mostly I like to *be* amused. See that dog behind me? He loves to tell jokes. Here's one: "Two pugs ran into a bar." Get it? Everyone loves to tell those smooshed-face jokes. Like I've never heard them before. Still, I love a good paw slapper.

Kiss kiss,
Homer

FROM THE DESK OF **HOMER THE PUG**

Dear Wilson,

I kept hearing how pugs shed enough to make a whole 'nother pug. It worked! This is my friend Furball. C'mon, Furball, I'll teach you how to become a wise pug so you can earn your yin-yang badge.

Wink wink,
Homer

FROM THE DESK OF **HOMER THE PUG**

Dear Wilson,

Today I met a dog named Astaire. He is not-a-pug. He is a guide dog for a blind person.
I remember what you said about not interfering or becoming a distraction. So I asked
Astaire how he would best like me not to interfere. He kept ignoring me, but since you
said it was important, I persisted until he finally paid attention to me.

I see what you mean, though—his human was being quite a distraction. She was making
such a fuss about crossing the street or something.

Astaire told me about how rewarding it is to help his human with her various projects.
I took this to heart.

Rock on,
Homer

FROM THE DESK OF **HOMER THE PUG**

Dear Wilson,

So I decided to help my human with a project. Astaire was right. It was quite rewarding.

Get down,
Homer

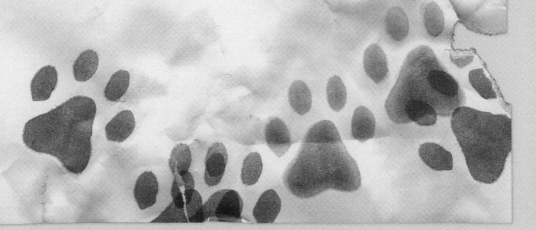

FROM THE DESK OF **WILSON THE PUG**

Dear Homer,

As we discussed, lessons are everywhere if you just look for them. See how the clothes drier is full of emptiness? Use this as a reminder. And whenever you see a household appliance, it will remind you to *apply* yourself.

With perseverance,
Wilson

FROM THE DESK OF **HOMER THE PUG**

Dear Wilson,

You really are very wise! I love using household appliances as reminders of our lessons.
I am finding new ways to apply my talents all the time.

Yum!
Homer

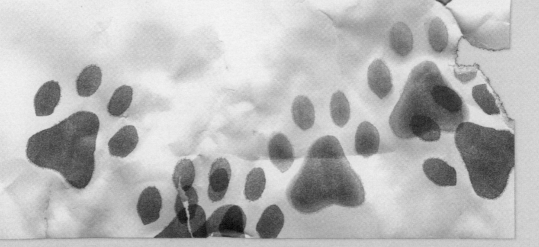

FROM THE DESK OF **HOMER THE PUG**

P.S. Fortunately, pug flatulence is no longer a problem for me.

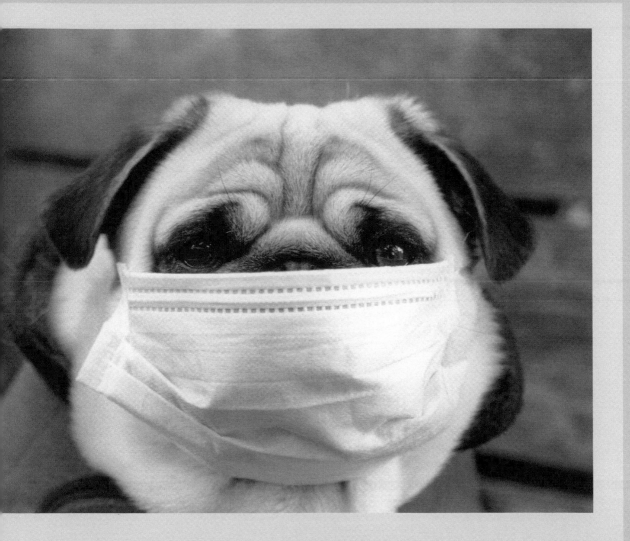

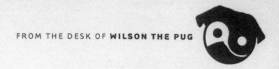

FROM THE DESK OF **WILSON THE PUG**

Dear Homer,

I would like to teach you about the ancient Chinese practice of feng shui. You'll notice that I achieve balance and harmony in my environment by stacking all the beds in front of the refrigerator.

With determination,
Wilson

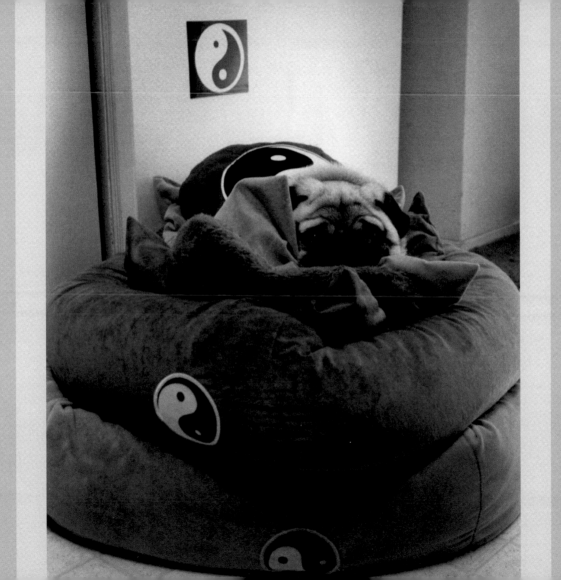

FROM THE DESK OF **HOMER THE PUG**

Dear Wilson,

Oh yes, I can see how this feng shui works wonders. With my bed *in* the refrigerator,
I feel more balanced and harmonious already!

L'chayim!
Homer

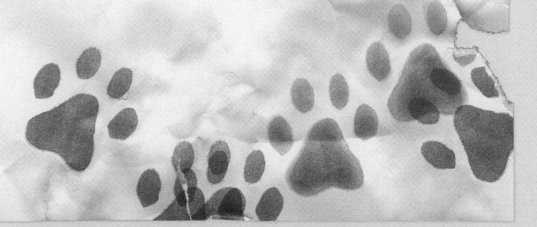

FROM THE DESK OF **WILSON THE PUG**

Dear Homer,

Pugs love to go for rides in the car, preferably a low-emissions hybrid vehicle, and only when absolutely necessary. And here's an important lesson: Even though it seems as if we were in control, truly, we are not.

With careening patience,
Wilson

FROM THE DESK OF **HOMER THE PUG**

Dear Wilson,

This is how I roll. Sixty miles to the gallon, too. And I go for rides only in mission critical situations. Like to get to a pug party. You're going, right?

Be there or be square,
Homer

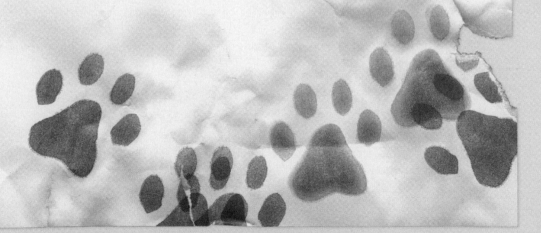

FROM THE DESK OF **HOMER THE PUG**

Dear Wilson,

Oh, I forgot to mention, it's my favorite sort of pug gathering. A pug toga party, otherwise known as a poga party.

Po-ga! Po-ga!
Homer

FROM THE DESK OF **WILSON THE PUG**

Dear Homer,

Thanks very much for inviting me to the poga party with your friends Morty and Inez.
It was enriching. Now, then, perhaps we can get back to our studies so you can become
a wise Taoist pug and earn your yin-yang badge.

With waning resolve,
Wilson

FROM THE DESK OF **WILSON THE PUG**

Dear Homer,

I sense that you may need some help sorting through the contents of my letters. I was happy to review them with you one by one. But what was that sawing sound?

With fortitude,
Wilson

FROM THE DESK OF **HOMER THE PUG**

Dear Wilsnoooorrrrrr . . .

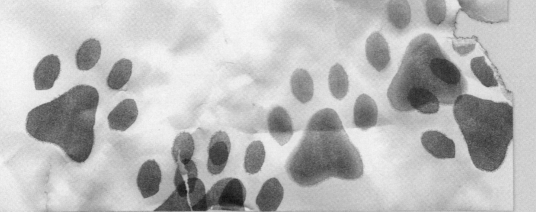

FROM THE DESK OF **HOMER THE PUG**

Dear Wilson,

I dreamed the giant bone was right on the table. It was so close but so far. And you were in the dream, trying to tell me something about the futility of obsessive desire. You were making no sense at all.

Giant bone, giant bone, giant bone,
Homer

FROM THE DESK OF **WILSON THE PUG**

Dear Homer,

I think we can use the ancient Chinese art of acupuncture to open your meridians and enhance the flow of chi, the vital life force. In this way, you can balance your yin and yang energies and fully embody the Tao.

Last try,
Wilson

FROM THE DESK OF **HOMER THE PUG**

Dear Wilson,

I have discovered a fabulous way to embody the yin and yang energies of the Tao.

Crunch time!
Homer

FROM THE DESK OF **WILSON THE PUG**

Dear Otto,

I give up. Enclosed please find my yin-yang jacket. I cannot pass along the wisdom of the Tao to young Homer. He will not be earning his yin-yang badge. I will not be assuming the leadership of the lineage, and I guess you will not be retiring to Boca after all.

Even though our twenty-five-hundred-year tradition will come to an end, I am at peace, accepting things as they are. I'm just me, Wilson the Pug, and I'm okay with that.

Your loyal protégé, always,
Wilson

FROM THE DESK OF **OTTO THE PUG**

Dear Wilson,

Just as I see clearly though I am blind, you may see your failure as success. You have passed the test I devised for you. For as it is written, "The Master can act without doing anything and teach without saying a word." When you gave up entirely and relinquished your yin-yang jacket without concern, you then became a true Master.

Young Homer has succeeded brilliantly at being a wise pug. Why? He is true only to himself. And this is true goodness. You will find his yin-yang badge enclosed with this letter.

My very comfortable throne becomes you. Now, then, I've got a plane to catch. After all, as it is written, "When you have accomplished your goal, simply walk away."

Your newly retired Master,
Otto

FROM THE DESK OF **WILSON THE PUG**

Dear Otto,

I am enjoying my new role, doing and saying nothing. And I know Homer is relishing the gift you sent him.

Your loyal Master,
Wilson

FROM THE DESK OF **HOMER THE PUG**

Dear Wilson,

Oh man, today I spent like four hours communing with the giant bone. You know, I think I saw this written someplace: "By being one with heaven, we become one with Tao."

Righteously yours,
Homer

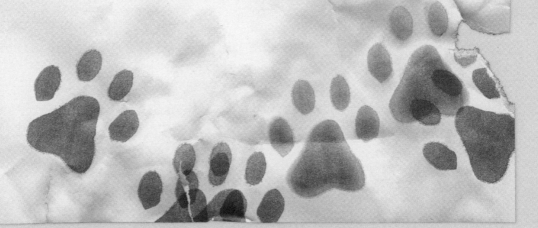

FROM THE DESK OF **HOMER THE PUG**

P.S. Oh and thanks for sending the yin-yang badge. It came with a great stamp. I could be wrong, but it almost tasted lemony with a hint of mint.

FROM THE DESK OF **OTTO THE PUG**

Dear Wilson,

I sit by the pool with an empty mind and a full glass. Life is good.

Infinitely and eternally yours,
Otto

Acknowledgments

"The highest good is not to seek to do good, but to allow yourself to become it."

—TAO-TE CHING, 38

From the bottom of our hearts, we'd like to thank the following good people for making this book possible: Our partners at Viking Studio, including Wilson's favorite and most trusted editor, Alessandra Lusardi, newfound champion Megan Newman, indefatigable Kate Stark, ever-steady Jessica Lee, always visionary Clare Ferraro, perseverent publicist Lissa Brown, and Daniel Lagin for the gift of his design. Special thanks to our good friend and Wilson's honorary godmother, our agent, Arielle Eckstut, and everyone at the Levine Greenberg Literary Agency.

For their generous cooperation, we wish to extend our deepest gratitude to Lisa Sheeran, Frisco Pugs, and the magnificently photogenic Otto, AKA Ch. Full Moon's Inphamous Otto, the incomparable Sally Shepard and Newman's Own® Organics, Dr. Ann-si Li and Assisi Acupuncture Ltd., Berkeley Dog and Cat Hospital, Pawsitively Gourmet, www.pawsitivelygourmet.com, for their delicious yin-yang cookies, Encina Veterinary Hospital, Dog's Best Friend & The Cat's Meow, Fritjof Capra, author of *The Tao of Physics*, with kind permission from Shambhala Publications, Courthouse Athletic Club, Sandi Thompson and Tater Tot, George (the pet store), Albany Medical Group, Thomas Lee Turman, Northbrae Properties, Mark and Susan Newman and Morty and Inez, and the spectacular Pug Fountain© Mark Newman Sculpture, newmanmark@sbcglobal.net, our friends at Guide Dogs for the Blind: Theresa Duncan and Astaire, Morry Angell, and Tamara Barack, and J. H. McDonald for his beautiful translation of the Tao-te Ching. Of course, special acknowledgment goes to Rainer Maria Rilke whose *Letters to a Young Poet* inspired our thoughts and title.

Thank you, LaMarr Desmond Medina, "the King of all Rottweilers," for the wonderful years of love and companionship. We will always miss you. For their kind support, we thank Lili Taylor and Gulliver, Tori Spelling and Mimi LaRue, Mary Steenburgen, Ted Danson and Roxy, Jenna Elfman and Gwen and Willy, Marv and Heather Albert and Lulu and Ruby, Kevin Keating, Alison Mann, MuchLove Animal Rescue, Sony Pictures Entertainment, and StopGlobalWarming.org.

We were once again lucky to have the privilege to work with a true master of her craft: Iris Davis of Davis Black and White. She breathes life into Wilson and friends. For their unwavering support and inspiration, we thank our circle of friends, especially Gregory

Hart Pinchbeck III. Thanks, too, to Wilson's original family, Myrna Powell and School House Pugs, and that of Homer, Jodi Sorensen and Treasure Pugs. Special thanks to Homer's best friend, Catherine Woodman. To Nancy's mother, Eileen Levine, late father, Irwin H. Levine, and sister, Fran Herault, we are grateful for your immutable place in our hearts and lives.